The Lake Remains

Poems by

Antonia Wilde

Cover image by Antonia Wilde
Author photo by Jeffery Daniel

ISBN: 979-8-90146-860-9

Kelsay Books
502 South 1040 East, A-119
American Fork, Utah 84003
Kelsaybooks.com

For Izzy

Praise for *The Lake Remains*

In *The Lake Remains,* Wilde's precise lines move like stones skipping across water, carrying the complicated poignancy of "dead flowers" that "spread rumors." Reminiscent of Kay Ryan's ability to turn the everyday into deceptively restrained, thought-provoking moments, these poems transform loss into reflections that ripple far beyond themselves.

—Candice M. Kelsey, author of *Another Place Altogether*

Antonia Wilde's new chapbook *The Lake Remains* is a story of grief and everlasting love that unfolds piece by piece. A dance between dream state and reality, Wilde's use of imagery draws out one's own grief with every turn of the page.

—Sara Rian, author of *As a Waterfall* and *Then Death Came*

The Lake Remains ultimately tells a story of love and how relationships can stand the test of time, even though physical presence might not remain. It's artfully crafted and takes you through emotional ups and downs that are relatable in so many ways.

—J.K. Kennedy, author of *Clumsy Beauty*

Contents

Author's Note

The Lake Remains is the story of an unbreakable bond between two souls. The story shares love through foundations of joy and, most prominently, through grief. While one soul may not remain physically, devotion does.

SHE'S THE ONE

The Forest Snow

I took you to the forest as a baby.
We walked bare, on all fours,
On the snowy pine-covered floor.
Snow clumped between our toes and fingers.
Prowling,
        Hunting.
                Jumping.
                        Joyful.

First Swim

The only way to learn how to swim is to be pushed
right off the cold white wood pier, into the crisp blue water.
A morning swim.
A ritual.
Rising sun, waves lapping, wind just barely there.
Push.
Together.

Wedding Dresses

Drove to the driftless region
And it smelled like yeast.
I drank the beer anyway.
I tried on dresses, but none of them fit.
I stared at the dense green hills
knowing, you would've run them, up and down, with grace.

And when the day arrived, you wore a champagne bow and;
I wore a champagne dress I found five minutes from home.

You did everything you were supposed to do:
Be by my side.
Sit at my feet.
Exclaim with joy.

After,
you went to the lake house
and I went to celebrate.

My heart was full, with you in it, grounding my night . . .
I was okay because you were okay.
I was okay because you were okay.

I was always okay with you there.

Ferndale

This was for you.

Acres to run, forests to explore.
Water to play in.
Food prepared, just the way you like it.

Babies to protect.
Siblings to share with.

Your corner to ponder—
where the sunlight hit the wood grain just right.

It was all too good to be true.
I just realized it too late.

Boat Rides

Sometimes the wind whips so strong, you can't hear yourself think.
Hair blowing so savagely, so delicate all at once.
Waves are destroyed underneath your feet.
Knees bouncing with the unruly tides.
The boat doesn't crack open,
but I do.

Time Escapes

I didn’t think you’d choose me.
But when you did . . . it all began.
Life, time-traveled 15 years at warp speed.
Zoom—zoom—zip—zap!
It all happened so fast,
an out-of-body experience,
like watching it unfold before you and then rewind.
Only . . . it happened to me, to us.
The births, the deaths, the fails, the triumphs.
And then,
you were gone.
All in one lifetime.

ICE PICK

Catapult Me

I take my time
stargazing into better days.
Hoping for the sky to fall on me,
and catapult me to wherever you are.

Tight Chest

The lake is holding its breath.
Frozen waves,
bubbles underneath.
That's how I love you.
Lungs tight,
bubbles underneath.
Waiting to see which feeling cracks first.

Fiore Cadavere

The dead flowers, next to my bed, spread rumors about me
while I try to sleep.
I beg them to whisper so I can have a modicum of silence.
Their voices roar, shaking my four walls.
“Sotto voce,” I say, “please.”
They howl—“We can’t hear ourselves over your thoughts.”
So, we all scream.

Masses

Unfortunately for me—
when I see you in my dreams—
I feel the Great Lakes between us.

Remorse

Contrition consumes me
and I am not religious.

Sorrow for sins?
I am in a state of guilt
over the knife that split under pressure,
that did you so wrongly

I let you walk down that hallway to another world,
at the sterile hands of a man who did you wrong.

Forgive myself?
That will never happen.
Just anger bouncing between forces,
torpedoing through the atmosphere.

I will die on this ship.
Sink in the lake, rudder and all.

Grief Is a Fisherman

Grief sways in the dangling branches of the lone willow tree,
green tips touching the water.
Grief flows effortlessly upstream with the speckled trout.
Grief balances on the stacked rocks by the shoreline.
Grief moves with the faired seaweed, each piece floating like
fingers through the water.
Grief bobs like the canoe waiting patiently on its buoy. Up and
down, side to side.
Grief hooks razor sharp into soft mouths with brightly colored
feathers flailing simultaneously.
Grief is a fisherman—steadfast in its craft, and;
Grief sinks me, like the red and white bobber is praying to stay
afloat.

RECEIVING

Gold

I can’t bear to lose you.
So, I’ll wrap you around my neck
and take you everywhere with me.

Insects

My dad is a tickling spider.
My dog is a fluttering butterfly.
My grandma, a humming bumblebee.
Together, they prance on the shoreline around me.

Earth Body

“She’s still with you,”
they whisper.

I don’t know how that can be when I am in my Earth Body,
and she is not with me.

Taking Form

She’s in the blue hues of my painting.
The pink flowers knew her best.
Her nose twitched after a sneeze, and her eyes glittered in gold speckles.
You cannot see her.
But her flame never went out.

The Leash & Lake

I'm in the house we dreamed of.
I can see the lake through the pine trees.

I saw you frolic down the hallway last night.
It was dark, but I knew it was you.

A shadow, a storm rolling in.
It's not calm on the lake—
ferocious white-capped waves.

I walk,
and I walk.

The lone leash sits hanging by the back door.

Carry On

What more could you ask for?
In this life,
beauty surrounds you.

Why do you let your troubles consume you?
Let them come and go.

Waves crash into the rocks.
Rocks scatter into sand.

She is in the stars, and;
the lake remains.

About the Author

Antonia Wilde is an emerging poet whose work explores the raw, unfiltered depths of human emotion and the natural world. This is her first published book of poetry. Her poetry focuses on grief, nature, longing, and becoming. She studied English Writing in college, earning a Bachelor's degree. Antonia's work is short, vivid, and punchy. You can find her writing by her favorite lake in Wisconsin, surrounded by her favorite books at the bookstore she owns.

www.ingramcontent.com/pod-product-compliance
Lightning Source LLC
LaVergne TN
LVHW020313110826
845148LV00017BA/2648

* 9 7 9 8 9 0 1 4 6 8 6 0 9 *